WHY MAN STILL KILLS MAN and FIVE STEPS TO STOPPING IT!

WHY MAN STILL KILLS MAN and FIVE STEPS TO STOPPING IT!

HUMANITY ESSAY SERIES

ROGER COLLEY

To order additional copies of this book, contact:
Xlibris Corporation
1-888-795-4274
www.Xlibris.com
Orders@Xlibris.com
51317

SYNOPSIS

Whether through natural evolution over a long period of time by chance or by design or whether through creation in His image by a Maker, Man by his very human nature has innate capacities for both aggressive behavior leading to brutal violence as well as altruistic behavior leading to compassionate caring. In either case, he behaves in ways perceived to be a gain in personal or group advantage. Foremost among immediate steps we can collectively take to end the most extreme forms of violence is a major revamping of the United Nations peacekeeping effort. Additional steps include a new program of worldwide electronic education; a greatly enhanced research effort to better grasp the workings of the human brain; assistance by the visual media in changing mindsets away from violence; a better way to channel natural competitive forces to the constructive good; and, a new dedicated use of advanced methods of resolving human conflict. The end result of this major movement forward will be to free substantially more resources to better solve other important problems pressing upon the world community.

PROLOGUE

Referral to "I" in the following essays is just "me" speaking in everyday language – a plain citizen of the United States of America and a single member of the world's human race. These initial three essays collectively entitled *Why Man Still Kills Man and Five Steps to Stopping It!* represent solely my opinion. While I have read and listened extensively about this subject matter, I have not documented my research. I have referenced some Associated Press news reports. I have also referenced some of the thinking of others but include no specific quotes. I can't read everything. I am not an authority. I am not an academic. I have no scholarly credentials except I do confess that I enjoyed magnificent guidance from very upright parents, am blessed with an excellent high school education, and have earned an Ivy League college degree. I have also benefited from forty years of sound business experience, many as a leader dealing with many different kinds of people in many different kinds of situations.

With that guidance, education and experience, and more recently from reading, listening and studying both recent events and the history of Man and his multiplicity of behaviors, I have arrived at this conclusion: while the peoples of the earth have multiple problems to deal with daily-economic disparities, lack of education, pollution, poor sanitation, poor water quality, food shortages, natural disasters, diseases, prejudices, injustices, inequalities and more – *at the very least at this stage in our human development we should be able to understand and stop the most serious of all destructive human behaviors – that of willfully inflicting violence one human upon another.* We thought it was the end of war after seventy million people perished during World War II and the subsequent creation of the United Nations. But no, not so in the sixty years since.

Lamentably, we are still seeking and striving for the end of gang violence, for the end of sectarian ethnic and religious killing, for the end of mass killings, for World Peace.

Many pacifist groups, hundreds of them, pursue this goal. Many great persons and worthy institutions laudably devote themselves to the promotion of "non violence", speak out boldly and perform many good deeds in this regard. They are to be commended and encouraged. Yet why, oh why, does the willful killing of Man upon Man still go on in this so-called "modern, civilized society of the peoples of the earth"? How do we stop it? Simply because it really bothers me that no one in a leadership position seems to have ready explanations with workable solutions, in the following essays I strive for my version of answers and solutions to the problem. I am not promoting an existing ideology, presenting a new one, or criticizing the many out there now. I simply feel we have an infinitely better chance to solve so many of humanity's challenges without the suffering, cost and destruction of willful human violence.

I plan to present these ideas to the public, to key decision makers and to persons of great influence. I then plan to follow up with more specific steps in future essays in this series. The aim is not another plea or expression of hope but a *call to action*. The chips will fall as they may – it's worth the try.

HUMANITY ESSAY SERIES

ESSAY ONE

IS YOURS THE SAME AS MINE?

'HUMANITY' seems to be taken for granted as meaning sympathetic and considerate to the dignity and worth of other humans collectively – you know, humane. But Webster's has a second definition of simply meaning the quality or state of being human. So there it is! The seeming paradox of why Man can kill a member of his own species, but also love him, can be explained. Within the vast complexity of our human natures comprising our diverse behaviors, your humanity therefore can be quite different from mine. Even so, despite our differences there are commonalities, and so I assert in these essays that there is great hope we can achieve that elusive goal that seems so common to most Man – the end of violence among peoples and World Peace among nations and within nations.

*   *   *

The news came over the radio on the porch of my friend's house. I remember it vividly. I was seven years old. The Japanese surrendered – the war was over. While lucky for me that my Dad was too young for the First World War and too old for the Second, I did have three uncles in World War II and remembered their letters as I played with my metal tanks and soldiers in the dirt outside. I had mixed emotions. I had thought war must be a bad thing as Uncle Tony was in a Nazi prison camp, Uncle Bob was injured in Iwo Jima and Uncle Art was on a boat to Germany, but at the same time I thought it was neat that our soldiers in those smart uniforms were winning against the bad guys. And then of course there were all those John Wayne war movies and westerns that always portrayed the 'good guys' beating the 'bad guys'. In my middle class family with two working parents striving to provide better housing and schooling for their children than that which they had grown up, my values were clear. My humanity was good. I wasn't going to hurt anyone. The inhumane bad guys were the ones who hurt and killed people, although I didn't understand why. Good and evil were clear cut to me, my family and my friends.

Learning that Jews were fighting Palestinians in 1948 seemed strange because I thought war was over. I had even heard of the newly formed United Nations. Then came more confusion as I found myself looking daily at the front page of our newspaper – there, the changing battle line in Korea. I was only 12 and then soon a young teenager – curious as to why men had to fight while, close by, men were "playing". Like my favorite Phillies playing the Yankees in the World Series in 1950. Nevertheless, to put an end to things in that far away battle, I couldn't understand why the famous General McArthur could not bomb the Chinese supply lines when our good guys were getting pushed back to South Korea in the freezing winter. Oh, China's ally Russia had the atomic bomb! So now we had Communism to deal with after defeating Fascism and Nazism. And talk of bomb shelters and nuclear warfare. And bad dreams. Confusing, this humanity.

*　　*　　*

Ten years later – all good ones for me – I had to put my mind back to war issues again. We had the draft then and close calls like the Berlin airlift and the Cuban missile crisis. In 1960, I signed up for six years in the US Air Force Reserve. The commitment for active duty was only six months, meaning I could return to a new job that I had started shortly after my college graduation. I was too old in the late 60's for service in the Vietnam War, which seemed like a line drawn in the sand to halt Communist expansion, or was it just a civil war? Whichever the argument, it clearly was a poorly implemented strategy to put young American boys to involuntarily seek and destroy natives where the good guys and the bad guys all looked alike and where the bad guys on their own turf were going to fight to the death regardless of the cost. Hmmm, idealistic America competent in World War II, seemingly incompetent in Korea, Vietnam and now Iraq.

As an international business executive in the 1970's, I pictured and experienced the world in three camps. Each revolved around its ideology. The Communist bloc wanted to dominate the world with its form of centrally controlled economies and its disregard for human freedom of choice. The Western countries, whether capitalistic or somewhat socialistic, espoused individual freedoms and friendliness towards the business community in advancing the welfare of all. The Developing and Underdeveloped nations were usually dictatorial and in the contradictious position of wanting American capital for advancing their economies but at the same time corruptly guarded in their allowance of free enterprise. During this time, I tried to hope the nuclear standoff between the US and Russia would prevail and that no "accidental" missiles would be fired that would trigger the end. That red phone on our leaders' two desks actually provided some real comfort as I went about my business and the raising of my family without daily fears. My occasional thoughts about "humanity" were limited to the hope that someday those around the world who suffered under oppressed leaders would find this wonderful treasured gift of individual liberty. It was still a "good guy-bad guy" mentality but with fervent confidence on my part that *reason would eventually prevail* and that the "good guys" would eventually win. Little did I ever think about the motives of those "bad guys", why they acted as they did, or even that some of them seriously believed that we Americans were really the "bad guys".

While my family and I thrived in the 1970's, I really cherished the 1980's with the collapse of the Soviet Communist bloc and a rebirth of the American capitalistic system – the latter a nice balance between the energies fostered by free enterprise as the engine and government as referee of the game and protector of the unable. We enjoyed a sigh of relief. The 1990's exposed some of the individual acts of greed and excesses that come with the territory, but overall our economic and political system has created such wealth for the overwhelming majority of Americans that ironically I feel our biggest problem economically now in America has become the spoiled consumer . . . Outraged at the slightest inconvenience. Obsessed with instant gratification. Unaware of how delicate in the balance of world events lies our success. Ignorant of history. Guzzlers of imported oil less expensive than domestic alternatives. Insatiable thirst for constant and expensive entertainment. But fortunately, full of vigor to try new things. Industrious. Innovative. Productive. Competitive. Compassionate. Free!

*   *   *

So now, at the start of a new century, our collective humanity in America turns to the great debate over protecting ourselves from certain so called radical or fundamentalist elements within certain sects of Islam. It seems ok to most parties in America to kill "terrorists" The questions are how and where. Why do they believe they have to impose their view of society upon others by force? They bombed the World Trade center in 1993 and vowed to come back again, but we didn't take it quite seriously enough with so many other issues in front of us and a disjointed intelligence network. We do pay a little attention to injured and starving children in Africa and some attention to a "nut" in North Korea who has the atom bomb but hopefully little motivation to use it. We do act compassionately with our "humanity". Our contributions are generous when sudden devastating natural disasters occur such as the tsunami in Asia and the hurricane of 2005 in Louisiana. By mid 2006, many of us became concerned about another "nut" in Iran potentially developing nuclear weapons as he makes public statements that Israel must be destroyed. Where is my old axiom that "Reason Will Prevail"?

From my little sixty year tale, one can see that Man killing Man did not stop in 1945 with the end of World War II when seventy million people died and prompted the creation of the United Nations to attempt to preserve international peace among nations. Millions more have died in violence since – all "civil" wars? Palestinians and Jews claiming the same god given land; North versus South Koreans; the killing fields of Cambodia; Northern Irish Catholics versus Northern Irish Protestants; North Vietnamese versus South Vietnamese; Lebanese factions; tribes versus tribes within the Congo, Somalia, Ethiopia, Uganda, Sudan; Shiites versus Sunnis in Iraq; Croats, Serbs and others in former Yugoslavia; Taliban versus non-Taliban in Afghanistan; rebels in Sri Lanka; rival ethnic groups within Pakistan and between Pakistan and India, Kurds in Turkey. Just irresolvable internal disputes over ideology, resources, control, religion? But then 9/11 certainly was no internal dispute. It seems we humans have competing goals, always good in the eyes of the beholder, but not always good at solutions to achieving them amicably. If we cannot agree on how to impose my cause or resolve this conflict, must I kill you? Can I get what I want only by using force?

*   *   *

What are we fighting about? Why? Why so much violence? Are we by our instinctive human nature fundamentally aggressive? Are we born sinners? Are we sometimes possessed by the devil? Or, is our "humanity" truly that of inherently being kind to others? Compassionate about human physical and mental suffering that brings others pain, tears, blood and death? Is it just unfortunately a few "inhumane" guys who are always causing all this killing here and there simply for one selfish reason or another? Or could it be that "humanity" is different within us and among us, part aggressive, part compassionate? *We are of being human.*

*   *   *

One well respected evolutionary biologist has put it to the effect that we have many human natures and that perhaps we can each and every of us show altruism and yet we can each and every one of us wreak violence. As John Adams was drafting our Constitution, his wife Abigail Adams cautioned her husband that every man could be a tyrant. Taking heed, Adams drafted a document calling for such an incredible balance of powers that, except for our Civil War one hundred and forty years ago, our nation of diverse immigrants has remained unbelievably stable through a sea of change in world events. With some notable exceptions to be discussed later, we in America live under an ingenious rule of law with the consent of the people that *generally* channels Man against Man on the playfield and in the courtroom and not on the battlefield. But worldwide and worrisome for all since the horrific events of 9/11, I feel a tremendous sense of urgency in the need to change the dynamics. We desperately need new ways to end the killing immediately. To do so then opens the door to incredible better opportunities to solve all the other problems Man faces.

*   *   *

15

Now that I see explanations for our variety of behaviors more clearly, I express thoughts in my second essay as to why I think in certain instances Man still kills Man. Happily in my personal outlook on life – the optimistic "the cup is half full" as opposed to the pessimistic "the cup is half empty" – you will find that my third essay will pile my own solutions to curb violence on top of all those already out there. On top of those that are not working, working to some extent, or haven't been tried yet. The devil is in the implementation, in the competent execution. Here goes. Thank you Abigail and John Adams and thank you General George Washington and our Founding Fathers for the opportunity for free expression.

*   *   *

Lastly to this introductory essay, I wish to express the thought that while I will continue to hold my own treasured personal convictions and values pertaining to whole host of subjects, on this universal topic of violence I speak as both a plain American and a plain human of the world. Hopefully the tone on this subject is transparent – not Republican, Democrat, Independent, Liberal, Conservative, Jew, Christian, Muslim, Buddhist, Hindu, atheist, agnostic, theist or any other specific label, but rather I speak out as a concerned citizen of the species *homo sapiens*. I want these Steps to stopping willful violence to work!

HUMANITY ESSAY SERIES

ESSAY TWO

WHY MAN STILL KILLS MAN

So why should we Americans care about it? Some 2.5 million Americans die per year, but only 18,000 of those from homicides. Most deaths are from health related disorders and disease and another 100,000 from accidents. We now spend a significant portion of our Gross National Product on healthcare and more and more annually on ways to reduce accidents. But homicides? Recently, a college professor had his remarks published to the effect that we shouldn't worry so much about our 3000 killed on 9/11 since it was such a relatively small number. Instead, we should spend our defense dollars on gathering foreign intelligence as a way of averting future threats. Others, including many prominent political leaders, feel we have no business meddling in civil wars overseas. As an example, since 2003 some 200,000 Sudanese have been killed in its southern area of Darfur while both the United Nations and the United States have not intervened to stop the civil violence. In the 1998 to 2002 civil war in the Congo, some four million persons lost their lives. Yet, on the other hand, it is interesting that in 1998 the President of the United States without specific United Nations resolutions ordered our military to intervene in the former Yugoslavia because the American public could not bear to watch on their television sets the brutal slaying of thousands of Muslims – so called ethnic cleansing. A civil war. We still have 15,000 troops there. Also it is interesting that we still have another 25,000

American troops fifty years later on the border between North and South Korea in order to prevent another civil war there. In Iraq – another civil war – do we continue to intervene or not? Some Americans say "yes" in order to at long last change the dynamics in that part of the world towards democracy and to prevent another Cambodian killing field. Others say "no – bring the troops home now".

This all sounds so confusing, doesn't it? Maybe we intervene only where the action promises to be quick, clean, and competent, like the 1991 Gulf War. But after the terrorist attack on the United States in 2001, we have been fully absorbed with homeland security and international terrorism. Do we have a dilemma here? Do we Americans have compassion with the act of Man killing Man or not? I believe we do, both of our own here at home and of others abroad. Do we Americans have cause for concern about potential future violence from weapons of mass destruction? I believe most of us do, as little as we like to think about it. Obviously I am on a mission to both understand the reasons for human violence and more importantly to find practical ways to stop it.

*　　*　　*

Murder is against the law in the United States. The traditional norms of our society find it detestable. Killers are hunted down and punished. The newly elected primary winner and most likely next mayor of my native Philadelphia won on his position to get tough in his approach to inner city violence. Because of this rule of law in our culture, most murders today are confined to inner city gang disputes, family disputes and mentally deranged individuals. Uncontrolled emotions like rage and anger or perverted beliefs or psychiatric illness are often cited as motivating factors. Ease in obtaining guns and drugs facilitate the resulting violent behavior. Much has been written about a young man's motivations after he recently murdered 32 students and faculty at his own university. More about these reasons later. Since the Civil War, there has been no general war mentality within our borders among Americans. We may engage in a war of words among ourselves, but we are *generally* at Peace among ourselves physically despite the most amazing mix of vastly different cultural backgrounds in our midst. Just look at New York City. Almost every culture in the world working and living together with only isolated incidents of violence. How so? Why not everywhere?

So I began thinking, with American troops still in both Korea and the former Yugoslavia and now actively fighting in Iraq and Afghanistan, along with all the recent killing in Africa, Israel, Palestine and Lebanon, there must be an explainable reason why this is still happening in this so called modern civilized world. The answer I find goes back firstly to the very basic nature of Man's inherent behaviors, and then secondly to the growing complexity and diversity of both our biological and cultural evolutions that have brought us to where we are today. And where we are today in this realm of human aggression and violence can be contained in just one day's series of headlines in just one city's newspaper printed September 14, 2006: "Drinking, Guns and Teens a Deadly Mix; People often Resolve Disputes with Guns; Friend or Foe in Fog of War; Amnesty Report Accuses Hezbollah of War Crimes; Dozens Found Dead on a Bloody Day in Baghdad; Man Kills 1, injures 19 at college in Montreal; US's Deadly Errors in Darfur."

To meet the challenge of reducing the thousands of horrible US homicides and the hundreds of thousands of cruel homicides abroad and to protect future generations from the advanced weapons Man has invented, we must first understand the causes of Man's behaviors.

*　　*　　*

Let's start with *humanity*: that is, human nature, humanity, the instinctive behaviors of Man, the learned behaviors of Mankind. "Man" meaning all within the human race. It matters not to my conclusions whether one accepts the scientific theory of the evolution of Man's start in life by sudden mutation, or by gradual natural selection or the by the sudden divine creation of Man by a supernatural force we commonly call God. The aggression, violence and killing among Man are inherent in either approach – whether traced to his evolutionary fight for survival or attributed to his original sin at his divine creation. In either case, one has a difficult time finding the whole Truth. In attempting to tell the real story, science has accumulated many facts in dated materials and fossil records, but the evidence is full of gaps and speculation. The science is incomplete. Likewise, the great religions of the world that attempt to explain who we are and how we should act are matters of faith not fact. Same with the great philosophers with their lofty explanations of human behaviors. All sides may proclaim the Truth, but yet it is hard to argue against the view that intense scholarly debate continues to reign within, between and among all these approaches. At best then, I am left in this endeavor to the best of my knowledge, my experience and my logic to express my pure opinion as I draw my own conclusions. *Any value to be associated with these ideas can only accrue if in time they become irresistible.* That is my great hope.

It is quite interesting that the world's major religions came about over a very short 3,000 year span [approximately 2500BC to 500AD], as Man's use of art, language and writing began to flourish. Also interesting that the major religions seemed to first give foremost attention to an orderly way that Man should live together, including both to his obedience to individual righteousness and to his care and compassion for others. Could it be perhaps that organized religions emanated as an answer to the inherent disorderly nature of Man who possessed by then an intellectual ability to think about, relate to, and write about his relationships with others as well as his own personal spiritual needs? God's word brought order and redemption. He brought a new sense of compassionate and moral behavior to sinful Man. In times prior, Man's pagan religions focused attention on supposed supernatural spirits believed to control the major natural forces. In that process, human life was often cruelly sacrificed to influence these spirits.

*   *   *

Science, on the other hand, tells a story based on the laws of physics and chemistry. Particles of matter, forces of energy and conditions. Physics – the four forces of electromagnetism, gravity, the strong force, the weak force and their play upon basic particles of matter. Chemistry – the varying conditions of pressure and temperature and their play upon particle combinations and their releases of energy. Some 15 billion years ago in the creation of our particular galaxy within the universe, particles of matter exploded and began to extend into space. The simplest stable atomic matter became what we observe as one electron revolving around one proton, each having an opposing electrical force, and called by us the element of hydrogen. Gradually coming together into a denser core, the conditions of chemistry then produced a fusion of hydrogen elements into higher level helium elements while releasing vast amounts of energy waves – it was a star. In time the pressure inside the star caused the next explosion again scattering matter. Some matter coalesced, cooled and attracted around a star's gravity in the form of a planet – like the Earth, some 4.6 billion years ago. The continued cooling effect of our planet eventually produced more complicated combinations of electrons and protons – over 100 elements, and then the combinations of these elements into a multitude of compounds. Chemistry continued – with further cooling, the elements of hydrogen and oxygen easily combined to form the water molecule leading to our clouds, rain and vast oceans. With the earth spinning like a giant turbine, electrical lightening filled the new nitrogen atmosphere. In the earth's waters a billion years later and with the introduction of the stable carbon element, all these actions somehow produced the conditions for the planet's first life to form – self replicating compounds of oxygen, hydrogen, nitrogen and carbon. DNA! Biology was born with one celled microscopic organisms containing instructional DNA molecules that could find an energy source and thereby reproduce themselves. Bacteria!

Over the next billion years, one celled algae multiplied in the seas. Their chemical metabolism of utilizing the sun's energy to sustain themselves released free oxygen to the oceans and to the atmosphere. To the benefit of new living organisms, the chemistry of combining oxygen with a vegetable food source, i.e., hydrogen and carbon, and converting them to sugar, resulted in a very efficient energy producer. Think of a match burning. In time, this respiration process produced the animal kingdom on earth – some 600 million years ago.

Of course there is still a great deal of mystery and speculation as to exactly how animals developed specialized cells within the organism – sensory cells, structure cells, nerve cells, organs and so forth. Some scientists suggest it was a sudden mutation in a set of genes that control structure. What is evident is that these multi cellular beings needed a control system to keep order and provide direction among all its parts so that the animal could move in order to find food for energy and find mates to reproduce itself. That control system was the central nervous system centered in the specialized neural – celled organ we call the brain. Eventually, ultimately and unquestionably, the brain of Man became the source of all the technology that improved the condition of Man as well as the source of all the weapons that harmed Man. *The brain is It* – the source of all our perceptions and resulting actions – the good, the bad, your values, my values, your behaviors, my behaviors, your human nature, and my human nature.

Over a vast amount of time, Darwin's theory of natural selection would allow for a tremendous diversity of plants and animals to evolve. Both random genetic mutations that conveyed advantages for survival, along with varying environmental conditions applying selective genetic pressures to adapt, combined to allow the survival of the fittest new form of organism. These advantageous adaptations were passed down genetically to the next generation. The incredible miracle of adaptation has produced the tremendous number of species that we see living on our planet today. This broad diversity of plant and animal life happened even though some event ended the reign of the big dinosaurs and most other large species of plants and animals only some 65 million years ago. At that stage in our planet's history, the mammals we know today then had their chance to grow in size, to diversify and to evolve into planetary dominance.

*   *   *

Now let's go to the *emergence of humans*. According to some evolutionary biologists, human like creatures walking on two legs [hominids] departed from their common ancestors – the apes and the chimps [hominoids] – along about five million years ago. Others believe the converse – that the hand walking ape families departed from an upright homo class; that a sudden mutation to a four footed mammal created an upright being as long as 21 million years ago. The science goes on. Either way, it is now known factually that the human genome, the DNA sequence of hundreds of millions of building blocks of gene encoding molecules found in the nucleus of each of our cells, is over 98% identical to the genome of the chimpanzee. Remarkable! But so different when it comes to our brain in its chemical composition and size. [In chemistry, our brain is much alike the dolphin's, and in size our brain is three times larger than the chimp's.] Hominids advanced in size and dexterity over the next several million years, but our brain didn't become the "big brain" until some 500,000 years ago when scientists believe we were "thinking" enough in a newer head shape to be called "homo sapiens". That's us. Some scientists believe a fish-oriented diet rich in certain fatty acids may have substantially contributed to such a remarkable brain development. Again, the science goes on.

But progress must have been slow because it wasn't until the so called "Great Leap Forward" some 50,000 years ago when Man created more advanced tools, art, communication and methods of transportation. He branched out of his homeland Africa to all corners of the world. He adapted to new environmental conditions – most noticeably his skin color, lighter to absorb required Vitamin D for bone strength in geographical locations where the sun's rays were weaker. Black, brown, red, yellow, and white. Diversity of thousands of simple but different cultures then had their birth.

Forty thousand years went by, and then the next great event occurred some 10,000 years ago, called the Agricultural Revolution. It was the start of the "civilizations" described in our history books. Most importantly, the introduction of food storage gave rise to the growth of a diverse number of rapidly evolving "sophisticated" cultures, societies that would generate great human advances but also produce great violent conflicts. In a fertile stretch of land in the Middle East, traditional hunter – gathers found a way to harvest nutritious crops of wheat and to domesticate tame animals like cows, goats and sheep for their milk and meat. Now all of a sudden there was a surplus of food, so much so that Man could find time to use his big brain and perform other tasks other than those for pure survival. Small communities were founded and grew thus creating the conditions for Man "in town" to use his big brain for developing languages, creating building materials, producing writing materials, making clothing, tools, items of trade and yes, weapons. Weapons. For millions of years living in small groups, Man, only when necessary in order to survive, had been fighting Man, families fighting families, tribes fighting tribes. Now in the new age of "civilization", more sophisticated Man could fight Man with more and more terrible weapons, cities versus cities, empires versus empires, and eventually religions versus religions, nations versus nations. Brutal and violent. It seems that opening and reading a history book about civilized Man is mostly a recital of wars, dominant leaders, and dates of conquests.

What is all this fighting about? *Religions* tell us it is because Man has an evil side, a disorderly side, a sinful side. The devil takes hold. But adding to the complexity, we are taught Man also possesses a spiritual side. Among all the mammals, only Man has the mental capacity to ask: "Who am I?" "What is life all about?" "Who and what is controlling all these forces around me?" "How should I behave?" "Am I alone, or is a spirit with me?" "Does my spirit survive?" At first, the new thinking Man believed pagan gods were supernatural beings who controlled the necessities of the hunt, water, fire, weather, love, and so forth. But eventually, being at times disorderly and selfish, Man needed more explanations and direction. In the region of the Middle East, we turned for direction and salvation to the Prophets, or to the Son, or to the Messenger of a monotheistic God. In Asia, we turned to a series of philosophic/religious combinations in seeking order and reason. Many religions and philosophies brought law and order, a sense of compassion for the disadvantaged, and the hope of redemption in an afterlife. Norms of behavior, morals, and values were codified culture by culture.

Today, some 1500 to 4500 years after their conception, these major philosophies and religions still exert a major influence over the daily lives of billions of people. The spiritual side of Man still exists – that thirst for needing and finding meaning, responsible behavior and orderly structure to life and its aftermath – Judaism, Christianity, Islam, Buddhism, Taoism, Confucism, Hinduism, and many more. At times that thirst for knowing could not be satisfied through acceptance of faith, and so the list of atheists is long – Aristotle, Hume, Voltaire, Paine, Santayana, Twain, Hemingway, Buck, Wright – smart men and women but still lacking all the answers.

* * *

So now let's go *back to science*, microscopic life, the plants, the animals and our brain. All those little viruses and bacteria that have been moving around for several billion years have only one cell. The virus is not even complete because it does not have enough genetic material to reproduce by itself so it must find a higher order host to help out. Bacteria reproduce themselves by simply splitting without a host's or mate's help. With only one cell they need no brain – just a food source for energy. Algae and multi celled plants also do not need a brain because they don't move; they just utilize water and the sun's energy to produce growth from available materials. However, the multi celled animals need a sensory system to move and find their energy sources, meaning their food, and to find their reproductive sources, meaning their mates. To accomplish this, we mammals all have eyes to see, ears to hear, noses to smell, mouths to taste, and nerve endings to touch. *A sensory system of nerve cells all controlled by the brain.*

So we now move to the results of having all those senses, that is, our behaviors, our natures, our actions. The smaller the brain, the smaller the number of capacities for possible behaviors, while the larger the brain, the larger the number of capacities for possible behaviors. The reptile has, let's call it, the Level 1 brain. Its sensory system simply helps it find its food, shelter and mate. It is on automatic pilot. It exhibits no emotions. It cannot reason. It is not mindful. Birds and mammals have, let's call it, the Level 2 brain on top of Level 1. Level 2 has an emotional response to sensory stimuli. These animals care for and protect their young. They show fear as well as triumph. Those closest to Man, the chimps, even display early behaviors found in the next level – let's call it Level 3, that sits on top of the first two. It is physically found on top front of our foreheads, our large cerebral neo cortex. Level 1 leads to automatic response behaviors. It is mindless. Level 2 is semi automatic; there is emotional feeling and some thinking prior to action. Level 3 is mindful. It separates Man from all the rest. It allows us to experience intense consciousness, heightened awareness, an ability to think with reason and logic, and to plan, organize and control events. It has allowed us to develop language to communicate with others, to say things to ourselves, to remember things, and to even write them down for preservation. The coordination among our brain levels in connection with our bodies gives rise to all the genius and talents we see in human activity today. It has also moved us beyond the basic instinctive survival behaviors found in all mammals – to a higher level to mindfully perceive emotions and events with an organized consciousness we call "reason". But before expounding on reason, let's go back again to earlier days.

*   *   *

Experience has shown that all the mammals, those big and strong animals that develop their young in a constantly nourished placenta and then feed on rich mother's milk after birth, exhibit the capacity towards violence, aggression and occasional death upon members of their own species. However, the stimuli for instinctive behavior to the point of killing are traced to only three competitive reasons: *one*, to fight over food; *two*, to fight over their mate; and *three*, to fight over their protected territory. Seems logical. One has to have food for energy, a mate to continue the species, and a protected area to rest and feel secure. The most basic of all needs. Fight to survive. But thank goodness, on the other side of the equation, in order to protect and nurture its family and clan so they too can survive, the mammals' basic instinct for caring is also forever ingrained. It is reasonable to assume that early man for millions of years was no different in his basic needs from the other mammals. The disorderly child, the caring mother, the strong father. Whenever needed, sensory responses sent to and from the brain with our hormonal chemicals automatically put our bodies into action to survive. The inseparable mind-body connection. Additional related behavioral actions simply evolved biologically as automatic instinctive behaviors, while many more complex behaviors later evolved in Man as the product of norms expected within our familiar group – our learned culture. So governing our behaviors today, we have experienced a long, slow biological evolutionary past and a more recent, more rapid cultural evolution. What is critical here to our understanding is that each of us inherently acted in *whatever behavioral pattern was advantageous to our individual and group survival and still do today.* Think about that. *To our advantage!!*

In time and with big brained Man evolving into larger societal groups with more advanced technologies, it seems logical in the *mindfulness of my big brain's Level 3* to understand how so many diverse human behaviors eventually developed. As pointed out, our individual senses of hearing, smelling, tasting, touching, and in humans especially seeing, trigger *Level 1 automatic impulses* leading to action or inaction in our behavioral responses. Like fight or flight. *Level 2 emotional perceptions* precipitate more complex feelings and behaviors and can also lead to behaviors that our Level 3 human brain can think of as rational or irrational ["rational" meaning experience teaching us observable and repeatable causes and effects of nonviolent, advantageous orderly behaviors]; or of value or valueless ["of value" meaning the norms of behaviors cherished as advantageous in each of our separate Man made cultures whether orderly or not, whether violent or not]. Our Big Brain today has vastly sophisticated those early basic drives for survival into a wide, wide array of behavioral possibilities.

*　　*　　*

Sound complicated? You bet it is! After millions of years of biological evolution and thousands of years of cultural evolution, *complexity* and *diversity* are the hallmarks in describing the human condition today. Each human being, all six billion of us, is ever so slightly different as a result of mixing our two parents' genetic blueprints together. We have slightly different individual biochemistries, each one of us, at birth. We then have different environmental and social factors affecting us as we grow. Despite a common ancestry or a common culture, with one trillion neural brain cells constantly sending out electrical and chemical messages in an age of vast bits of information available to us, we are bound to have differences of opinion each and every one of us! And brain wise, despite the same basic genetic blueprint constructing the same looking organ to the naked eye, each one of us does have a slightly different final atomic scale brain configuration. *Our world is populated by six billion different human brains!!*

We must also realize that genetic reproduction is not perfect. Some of us have inherent or environmentally caused defects at the molecular level in our brain chemistry or wiring that can lead to what we call pathological behavior – helplessly outside the norms of our particular culture. Many of us can have a perverted mentality based on prior mental history and/or affected disorders at the cellular level that cause inappropriate responses in behavioral responses compared to the norm. When we add the effects on our minds of the rapid and diverse cultural evolutions over the last 10,000 years through thousands of different societies then combined with modern day stresses, we can understand even more how different our human behaviors have become. How difficult a job it is for psychologists, psychiatrists and neurologists! How common our ancient past, how different our civilized present!

*   *   *

Can we risk simplifying all this to gain some clarity to the feature point of this essay? Yes, we can. What do we think are the common traits, common drives, and common instincts in this wide variety of human natures? Certainly the original *big three stimuli that could give rise to aggression – food, sex and territory* – were so important early on and are still evident today. But as stated, our behavioral action now takes place in such more sophisticated ways due to our Big Brain. Aggression over the search for food expanded to the drive for additional resources that can make life more comfortable. To the victors go the spoils. With the new supply of stored food and new weapons, aggression over protecting one's little territory of comfort and security expanded to aggressively acquiring resources of value in distant lands and peoples. While violent aggression of males over the competition for female mates has been subdued in recent centuries in many parts of the world, its subtle carryover can still be seen in the struggle for women's rights in many countries today. Today, mating competition that springs from the sensory emotions often takes the form of bitter jealousies, possessiveness, rivalries, anger and other passions that lead to painful disruptions to family life. Yet in many societies, rape and spousal abuse still continue to be major issues. In the Central African Republic, the UN reports tens of thousands of women have been raped by different factions in a country of little law and order. In February 2007, Mexico passed a law designed to curb domestic violence against women after the Mexican Health Ministry reported that about one in three women suffer some form of domestic violence including 6000 deaths per year. In my native Philadelphia, the FBI has reported 1,024 forcible rapes took place in 2006.

Fortunately, in this picture of complex aggressive instincts and drives is the *other side of the coin.* Early Man also protected his mates, family and group with the emotions and resulting *behaviors of love, cooperation and altruism.* To repeat an earlier point, it seems key that wherever there was an *advantage* to a certain behavior for purposes of survival, that trait became ingrained. That's the key word – personal ADVANTAGE. On the one side, within an early group typically composed of the dominant male and submissive others, that male's aggressive and violent behavior within his own species at times could have been essential to the welfare and survival of himself and his group; whereas on the other side, his altruistic behavior at times evidenced by loving care and cooperation would have been essential for his or his group's survival. We are, by the natures of us, a mixed bag! In time and with experience in the use of his hands and mind, Man advanced in mental complexity and sophistication. Debates exist whether Man's big brain gradually developed as a natural selection process in moving from the trees to the less protected savannah, or whether his particular seaside nutrition suddenly conferred an advantage in growing more brain tissue, or whether it was due to some unknown sudden event, but it happened. Early Man's basic drives that I have described became embedded in the unconsciousness of his mind, and later ritualized in his conscious mind within his particular group culture, meaning the norms of his select society. Within his own group's value system, such aggressive or altruistic behaviors could be thought of as good or evil, righteous or unjust, moral or immoral, ethical or unethical, virtuous or perverse, honest or dishonest and many more. In all these opposite side of the coin behaviors, remember that initiation of any behavior was originally perceived to an *advantage* to the perpetrator. Understandable! But also remember that by large, the over whelming majority of Man sided with the caring plus side of these behaviors because the plus side brings feelings of pleasure and comfort to our nervous system while the violent negative side brings feelings of pain and suffering to that system. The renowned philosopher Kant could not understand how a man of reason could ever want to harm another human being. However, understanding the biological history of the natures of Man and his more recent institutionalized cultures, if to his perceived advantage, we have even seen one human brutalize another and yet think it is righteous. Yes, our humanity can be different, but if I can try to simplify: [1] we commonly do what we do to gain advantage for ourselves or our group, ultimately in a manner to achieve comfort rather than pain; [2] under the rule of rational law, mankind tends to behave orderly, peacefully aggressive and most often caring. Unfortunately, killing others to achieve goals of advantage has periodically still been part of that modern Man's equation. My answer to Kant would be: "You are right, while we must all *feel* with our emotions, we must all *act* with our reason".

* * *

So, while Man is now "sophisticated", his advanced brain nevertheless spins in a wave of *Level 2 semi-mindful emotions that most often overrule Level 3 mindful reason*. The smartest of us still tend to easily expound his emotionally based "spin" or "slant" on just about any subject matter. His values are confused as he thinks about the opposing behavioral aspects of love and hate, tolerant and biased, just and unjust, fair and unfair and descriptions that go on and on. Socrates, Aristotle and Plato got us thinking about all this, and their thoughts briefly created Greek city-states that attempted to bring some peaceful reasonable order out of all these opposing natures. Soon, the likes of the inspired minds like Tao, Confucius, Buddha, Abraham, Moses, Jesus, and Mohammad helped lead the way to the orderly compassionate plus side of the ledger through their appeal to reason or to the love or fear of God's word. Nevertheless, on the negative side, as human societies grew larger and travel became easier, conquests of others became larger in scope and in brutality. Religions became institutionalized, sometimes irrational, sometimes violent. Cultural and religious values usually justified the violence. A dominant few individuals – no different than early Man, to militant societies, to today – usually led the way. With some brief exceptions, in growing societies the Dominant Male ruled – within the Greeks, the Persians, the Romans, the Christians, the Muslims, the Chinese dynasties, the Vikings, the Turks, the Nazis and so on and so on. This is a very important point: as the size of societies grew, our behavioral differences created stratification. We then see human layers of rich and poor, haves and have not's, kings and slaves, etc. Additional fuel for additional violence.

With Man's increasing numbers and his new ability to communicate effectively and develop new useful technology, it appears order could only be established through [1] the reasonable minds and influence of philosophers, [2] the directives of the dominant person in the form of tribal leaders, dictators, kings, emperors, caliphs, etc and [3] the laws of God emanating from all the new religions. Piled in this mix of chaotic conquest by the few versus order, peace and compassion for the many, an incredible amount of diversity ensued. Thousands of cultures evolved around the planet each having their own sense of norms, values, practices, beliefs, order and interpretations of right versus wrong. In that diversity of behaviors inherent in one of us, the violently repressive always faced violent rebellion from the repressed – a never ending cycle. From a few million humans at the start of the Agricultural Revolution 10,000 years ago, to 250 million at the time of Christ, to 6.4 billion today, Man has come to dominant the planet. *By understanding the various explanations of evolutionary biology and by understanding the origins of the world's dominant religions and cultures, one can begin to make sense of all the aggression and violence that continues to this day.*

*   *   *

With this background, and I know how repetitive I have been to reinforce my points, what I am expressing is that *Man has the mental capacity at all three levels of his brain to act in physical ways to secure an advantage.* Automatically, emotionally and mindfully, he behaves or has the capacity to behave to his own, or to his group's or to all of mankind's perceived advantage. That is his humanity. Over all the other mammals that have our same organs, it is Man's superior brain that is responsible for all the progress we have made in utilizing the planet's resources to our advantage these last 50,000 years, these last 10,000 years, and these last 200 years. Nevertheless, despite our vast and rapid technical advances to improve the human condition and our numbers, the rate of progress has been mixed, and many on the planet today suffer from war, conflicts, poor quality water, malnutrition and lack of good sanitation. It is *Man's superior brain* that endows us with the capacities for both the joy of caring and the agony of willful pain. Despite modern explanations for either our pathological or our normal motivations, our early drives have given all of us the *capacity* to inflict damage one upon another, and they are still recessed with us today in our genetic makeup. In the 21st century, one human killing another may not seem to stand to reason, but it is so, and it is explainable. In addition to our individual genetic behaviors, the evolution of human cultures magnified similar capacities on a collective basis. In many cultures, the warrior was and in many cases still is an exalted figure. A hero. Even most Christians believing in the non violent teachings of Jesus justify killing in self-defense. Some interpretations of Islam preach that the heroic warrior, the heroic martyr, earns a short cut to Paradise. Today, Muslims are killing Muslims just as 500 years ago Christians were killing Christians. Each sect feels justified and has its heroes and martyrs. In America, the tough brave cop and the tough brave gang leader are held in high regard by their peers. Many of these aggressive behaviors also become instinctive within common groups – the herding instinct. Remember the thousands of followers of Hitler.

* * *

In reviewing this maze of Man's history, it is clear to me that while some may claim they have all the answers, I submit that it is impossible for even the most learned scholars around the world to have The Whole Truth in their grasp. Despite this shortcoming, *I venture my opinion that all humans can experience the "good" emotions of feeling pleasure and happiness, and that all humans can reach the conclusion that Man, using his reason, prefers comfort over horror.* Therefore, it is reasonable to me based on observable experience, that every human on earth has, or has the capacity to develop, the mind set to experience pleasure over pain, happiness over sadness, peace over war. Why, because pain and sadness is our central nervous system telling us something is wrong. If wrong, then *is there a way to the ADVANTAGE without inflicting pain?*

The answer is "yes", but it is not so easy. In a small number of cases involving persons with severe mental imbalances, pain is actually sought out as a remedy for themselves or to inflict upon others. The young man at Virginia Tech, Cho, experienced inner mindful pain his entire life. Acclimated to the violence portrayed in our media, finding it easy to acquire advanced weapons, knowing he was not long for his suffering life on earth that he perceived the fault of others, he then perversely achieved his essential recognition by taking the lives of 32 fellow students and faculty with him as revenge. To achieve his ultimate advantage, he had to inflict pain on others he blamed. Joy/Pain. Isn't it interesting that when we feel pain our face grimaces while when we dance with someone we like our face smiles. Cho grimaced and never felt joy. His emotions and then his mind and then his body proceeded from a grievance to depression, to rage, to revenge, to the end.

Simple Early Man killed Man because of conflicts in his fight for survival. Complex Modern Man still kills Man because within his now recessive genetic instincts or subdued sinful soul his advanced mind has not yet learned to control his negative emotions, has not yet found a better way to settle conflicts., or has not yet reconciled how to transfer his fundamentalist beliefs to others in a peaceful way. At times, his basic instincts overrule his learned inhibitions. Alternatively, he rationalizes destructive behavior as of value and righteous, or has pathological brain chemistry, and quite simply has found that advances in weaponry make killing so very easy. Over the last 3000 years, Man's cultural evolution has far exceeded the pace of his biological evolution. Many of these cultures incorporate certain forms of violence into their norms, their values. And lastly, still going on today, is the ancient behavioral aggression of repressive dominant males over their submissive followers [or herding instinct followers] leading to violence in their rise and violence in their fall. Saddam Hussein.

One would think Level 3 Reason, based on the practical lessons and logic of observable cause and effect, would prevail today in the behavior of civilized humans, but all too often Level 2 Emotions win out as the dominant force in resolving conflict. Neuroscientists can today demonstrate that messages from our sensory system first visit the part of our brain controlling emotional behavioral responses before proceeding to the rational portion of our brain. Thus, today's school killings, gang killings, civil wars, genocide, religious killings, and ethnic cleansing all become irrational acts of the mind to the most of us, but to the perpetrators they are valid emotional responses to causes justified in their minds at the time. As examples, witness the terror today in August 2007 on the streets of Baghdad, or think about the 40 murders per day in the United States, mostly on the streets of our major cities. The news came March 6, 2007 that 140 pilgrims on a journey near Baghdad to mark a religious observation were murdered by a rival sect. News on March 17 of one 14 year old California boy stabbing another to death in gang war followed by a fellow gang member beaten up by his own members for running away – punishment by his mates for losing his gang honor. Then, March 24, 19 Sunnis killed by Sunni suicide bomber in Baghdad for collaborating with the government. On May 12, a sixteen year old Pennsylvania youth stabbed his best friend and his victim's parents to death in their bedrooms in the middle of the night. Friends stated the teenager seemed to have two sides to him! Can you look into the minds of these killers?

*   *   *

In conclusion, it seems evident to me that if we place just one more person next to the first, based on conditions at hand which may offer an advantage to either, conflict has the potential to arise from natural capacities to react aggressively. Or conversely if we add that one more person, love has the potential to arise from natural capacities to react cooperatively and compassionately to their mutual advantage. Our capacities for behavior can go both ways. Since our Big Brain's cerebral cortex has the ability to think and translate negative emotional responses into instigating violent behaviors, so too can our Big Brain find solutions to the problems of the relatively small number of people responsible for today's violent aggression, or more importantly for tomorrow's potential aggressors armed with small advanced weapons capable of immense destruction. With an extreme sense of urgency, we, Man, **must settle conflicts without violence**. We do have the capacity to do so. We do need a new MINDSET and we need to ACT! That action is the subject of the next essay.

HUMANITY ESSAY SERIES

ESSAY THREE

AND FIVE STEPS TO STOPPING IT!

We have learned that Man by his nature has inherent capacities to behave unto his own kind both in violently aggressive ways as well as with loving care. Whichever behavior to whatever degree as being most advantageous at the moment. Evolutionary biologists and evolutionary psychologists also believe in what one might call the 'Dominant Male" to have been essential to the welfare and survival of human groups over hundreds of thousands of years of early Man. And looking back over our recent recorded history of the last five thousand years, we see that it has been the "Dominant Male" who led the way in the major fields of war, religion and philosophy. With respect to war between nations, one could argue optimistically that things are now looking up as individual power has become more diluted. After the devastating World War II ended in 1945, a war that was responsible for the killing of seventy million people, a United Nations institution was founded expressing the noble goals of both eliminating war between nations and espousing the dignity of every human being. It was reasoned that representative governments that limited the power of any potential dominant tyrant would be less likely to start wars among nation states. Twenty democracies then have now grown to one hundred and twenty, some progressing and some regressing, but nevertheless a substantial step forward compared with fifty years ago. The highly militaristic defeated societies of Germany and Japan were forced

34

to change their collective mindsets, and their representative governments have been peaceful democratic models ever since.

Despite these advances, the killing fields in non-democratic societies continued. The worse outcome was prevented only because the thrust for worldwide domination of dictatorial Communism was stopped through the prospect of mutual nuclear annihilation. Détente. Nevertheless, the likes of ethnic tensions, cultural clashes, disputes about possession for old lands, irresolvable divides among religious factions, disputes over power sharing, conflicts over economic resources, and gangland feuds have all been responsible for the continuation of the killing of millions of people since the UN was established. The Cambodian killing fields of Pol Pot appall. Repressive governments still abound. Radical groups advocating their position only by force are still in our midst. Much worse, technological advancement in the destructive power of very small weapons makes the potential capability of an incredibly few number of potential killers of Man in the future a horrifying prospect.

If a Dominant Male were always leading the way, it would sound easy to end all this by eliminating any potential violent Dominant Male leader that arises, but that is not so easy. Who intervenes preemptively? Or upon the sovereignty of a nation? Despite academic and public declarations to the contrary, there is no *natural* drive within each human being either for freedom and democracy or even for consistent ethical behavior. We established that in Essays One and Two. Natural drives govern behavior leading to personal or group advantage. It is just that societies are more peaceful for all their members collectively when democratic non tyrannical conditions can be established, and it is just that an individual is always more "comfortable" or "happy" when no one is aggressively pressing upon him mentally or physically or expropriating his resources. He then has the liberty to utilize his creativity, his talents and the vast potential of his mind, all stemming from his big brain, in positive ways. Conversely, to limit our negative ways, laws by consensus spelling out wrongful behaviors in democratic societies keep "free" Man in check, while laws by the Dominant Male in dictatorial societies keep "subservient" Man in order. Nevertheless, crisis after crisis continues, the latest as I write this witness the murderous sectarian violence in Nigeria, Sudan, Afghanistan, Gaza and Iraq along with the threat of Iran possibly working its way towards building nuclear weapons even though it is a signer to the Nuclear Non-Proliferation Treaty.

Foremost in the battle of ideas today is the tug between the free mind in our liberal democracies versus the mind's complete obedience to a selective interpretation of God's laws in certain sects of theocratic movements. After this one, who knows what the next struggle shall be. In all of this turmoil, the challenge in settling conflicts without violence will be *first* to use our incredible brains to use Reason, which as I described in Essay Two can only be considered "good", and *second* to change the cultural Values of those who consider willful violence acceptable.

Use Reason, Change Values. URCV. That is the credo here on this one value – the RIGHT TO LIFE. Reason – nothing original here. We have had many Ages of Reason before, but at present we have to go beyond thinking about it and **do something about it**. My FIVE STEPS FOR STOPPING IT take into account the conditions necessary for both establishing each human's right to life as well as maintaining it. *There is no new human nature evolving here, no time for that, just initiating emotional responses to then use the reasoning power of our big brain to create new mindsets. In our natural drive to behave in a way advantageous to ourselves individually and to our identified group, we must find ways to obtain mutual advantage and to settle natural conflicts without killing each other.*

I enumerate the *FIVE STEPS* below and then will briefly amplify upon each one. Future essays will delve more deeply. Each action STEP is worldwide in scope:

1   **Enforcement of the Rule of Law of Human Life**
2   **New Directions in Education and Research**
3   **Media Blackout of Willful Violence**
4   **Refinement/Redirection of Competition**
5   **New Initiatives in Conflict Resolution**

1.   ENFORCEMENT OF THE RULE OF LAW OF HUMAN LIFE

The United Nations often receives criticism for not being sufficiently effective. Witness today's headlines: After ten years as Secretary-General of the UN, retiring Kofi Annan bids farewell with deep sorrow over today's widespread human rights abuses. Just recently seen on national television, actress Mia Farrow laments the UN inaction in the Darfur region of Sudan where she is volunteering her assistance. Over 500,000 killed and 2.5 million persons displaced. More recently, the UN attempts to place 26,000 troops and support personnel into Darfur while Sudanese government leaders express "neo-colonialism". Again recently, a nationally syndicated journalist laments the UN Security Council's silence over the hostage taking by Iran of British sailors. He writes that UN Council permanent member Russia enjoys superpower America becoming stressed in the Middle East and that Council permanent member China is dependent on Iranian oil. So, no action. But let's think about it more inventively.

The United Nations was created with lofty goals at a time when the world was weary of a devastating World War, but also at a time when many different opposing political systems, state ideologies, and cultural societies continued to exist post WW II. Is it not at least amazing in the long violent history of Man that just sixty years ago the signers to the UN Charter all expressed the wonderful goal of opposing war among nations? In order to quell major violence, it even created a 17-member Security Council that could resolve to intervene militarily if its five permanent member states could agree. Wow, look at that Charter. "We the Peoples of the United Nations United for a Better World". Its Preamble: "We . . . are determined . . . to save the succeeding generations from the scourge of war . . . to reaffirm faith in the fundamental worth of human rights, in the dignity of the human person, to establish conditions under which justice . . . can be maintained . . . and to these ends . . . to practice tolerance and live together. To ensure peace and security . . . that armed force shall not be used save in the common interest . . ." Wow! That is wonderful, and the facts are that since that signing on June 26, 1945, few wars have taken place between nations. Most have arisen as a result of civil and religious strife within nations, events the UN understandably was poorly equipped to handle. Interfering within a sovereign nation is a touchy subject: for example, Sudan, Korea, and the turmoil in Iraq. Interfering prior to actual violence is another difficulty, for example the British sailors captured by Iran without a shot being fired.

In Chapter 1 Articles 1 and 2 of the UN Charter, it is recognized that the institution's scope is "international" and that . . . "Nothing contained in the present charter shall authorize the United Nations to intervene in matters which are essentially within the domestic jurisdiction of any state . . ." Yet, on December 10, 1948 the United Nations General Assembly unanimously adopted and proclaimed the Universal Declaration of Human Rights, nonbinding of course, but listen to its Mission: "Human Rights First believes that building respect for human rights and the rule of law will help ensure the dignity to which every person is entitled and will stem tyranny, extremism, intolerance, and violence." And in its Preamble: "Whereas recognition of the inherent dignity and of the equal and inalienable rights of all members of the human family is the foundation of freedom, justice and peace in the world." What's wrong here? A United Nations Human Rights Council was even formed to promote and recommend actions in this area. To its credit, the world has ended up with lots of UN peacekeeping missions. Not the best trained or most effective, but in numbers there are over 15 missions right now employing nearly 100,000 troops from 109 different countries. We can assume many lives have been saved; yet the fighting goes on. The UN cannot effectively keep up with civil strife. Is it that we cannot all agree on what is a human right? On what is meant by human dignity? By who defines what is a rule of law? That we cannot interfere in domestic affairs? While UN employees and devotees may agree on human rights, seems not so for all our six billion people. The world is still ruled by sovereign states with the best protection of human rights in those states with stable democratic governments. Change comes slowly to the others and with much difficulty. But optimistically, maybe it is only a handful of individuals rather than states who are responsible for the violence. Let's see.

Despite our complex big brains each one so slightly different, despite our many human natures giving rise to a vast array of instinctive behaviors, and despite our many manmade diverse cultures directing many more diverse behaviors, let's go on to look at the 30 Articles of the UN's Human Rights, a wonderful outcome forged after much debate and compromise. Astonishingly, there was eventual agreement on these Articles by the myriad of diverse authors and signers. No, I think they are too utopian-impossible. Wishful thinking. It's heaven on earth. So let's just look at the all too important Article 3: "Everyone has the right to life, liberty and security of person". If all the nations of the world signed off on this thought, then LET'S ENFORCE IT! It is the most fundamental of all *reasonable* goals. It is the one universal value perhaps we can all agree upon. It is truly good over evil, as 99.9999% of us would in the modern world define those terms. That leaves only 6,000 really "bad" group leaders around the world that foster mass violence and persuade their followers to follow course! Leaving out for the moment those of us with severe mental disorders directing a path to violence, is this my "Bad Guy Dominant Male" number?

Of course, on the path to justice we can and should promote other goals as well, all of which lessen the need for civil disorders to be initiated by these group leaders in the first place. For instance, in 1999 the UN established its Culture of Peace with eight Action Areas, as outlined:

1 Education
2 Economic and social development
3 Promoting respect for all human rights
4 Equality of men and women
5 Fostering democratic participation
6 Advancing understanding, tolerance and solidarity
7 Communication and flow of information and knowledge
8 Promoting international peace and security

Good stuff! Did all the UN members sign that declaration? But what is really going on now. Recent morning news reported in Iraq: "A suicide bomber driving a truck loaded with TNT and toxic chlorine gas crashed into a police checkpoint in western Ramadi . . . killing at least 27 people and wounding dozens" while later on national television, a US Congressman said to the effect that we should pull all US troops out of the Middle East if a reason cannot be given why we should be there. Remember we still have 25,000 American troops in Korea preventing a civil war and another 15,000 in Kosovo preventing a civil war. Try this reason Mr. Congressman: after 2500 years of horrific wars in Western Europe, the mind set there now is "no more fighting". Accordingly, if after 2500 years of horrific wars still going on in the Middle East, cannot the UN wishes stated above give valid reason for the United States and others to help bring them to an end? In this age of advanced mass weapons, if it is only a few thousand "leaders" in Algeria, Nigeria, Chad, Sudan, Lebanon, Palestine, Iran, Syria, Sri Lanka and elsewhere [and some would even argue the United States!] who convince followers of violent means to securing what they believe to be righteous, should not the smart six billion Man find other ways for them to settle grievances and conflict? Yes, but first we need an enforcer.

Speaking as an American, clearly the United States cannot and should not act alone as the world's policeman. Even with all the problems within America still needing to be resolved, for example illegal immigration, the United States undeniably has been a major force in helping the lot of Man everywhere over the last hundred years. Despite some critics who incredulously argue that it is America which is responsible for today's turmoil, our image and influence could be immeasurably enhanced through my proposal. The step that I am promoting here is a radical move forward in international relations. If everyone truly were a "good guy", there would be no need for armed force to preserve order.

We know that is not the case. All societies require law and order. How do we accomplish the task? *First, we need to regroup and revise the UN Charter in the incredibly difficult task of redefining international strife.* For UN intervention to be called into action, armed conflict must include not only strife between nation-states, but also strife of a certain magnitude within nations. We need to go beyond the modest UN "peacekeeping missions" now underway. One would cringe that the criterion might be so many deaths inflicted prior to intervention, but some measure or some common definition of genocide can be negotiated. Certainly I do not mean that internal police actions against a small number of domestic "criminals" would require UN intervention, but I would except those cases where the small number engage in *international* killing and local police actions have proven insufficient. But let me not get into those details now – the *second task is that we need a strong international enforcer*, and logically under the banner of a revamped United Nations Charter and Security Council.

For starters, *the new enforcers would be the Big Three – the United States, Russia and China*, and of course any additional volunteers. Probably, Britain and Australia would selectively join. Perhaps France under its new leadership. A nation from Africa, South America and the Middle East. Would it not be even great if Iran ended its support for militant groups and selectively joined as an important player on the world stage of UN objectives? The Big Three. The SuperForce. Preposterous! Crazy? Not so. The once Nazi Germany and Imperialist Japan are now American allies as model democracies, but not armed. Our armed former Communist adversaries, Russia and China are undergoing major economic and political transformations. Russia appears concerned it has lost superpower status, and this step would be a major breakthrough in the psychological uplifting of its government and its people. The nation becomes important again in a whole different but admiral way. China, the once sleeping giant, has awakened and is taking peaceful steps as an international player in order to obtain raw materials for its rapidly developing economy. Why not also become an international "good guy"? There is no reason to believe that for Russia and China it is not to their significant advantage to enjoy a more peaceful world and to be elevated to the status of international Superpowers. They have learned that the way to their future prosperity is in peaceful trade not war. It is said that economics is the basis of politics. I believe good economics is the basis of good politics. If this thinking is the most advantageous to the most people, we should and can move in this direction. Underlying any such notion obviously implies a peaceful, non-violent world. If the UN needs a Super Three Plus police force as a step in accomplishing such a goal, then so be it, let's do it. It is my guess that even the populace support for the militant organizations of the Hamas and Hezbollah has as its basis the improvement of the economic status of its followers as much as the religious factor.

Probably too late for President Bush, President Putin and President Hu Jintao to consider, but in the coming months, I will be dedicating myself to expounding upon and finding practical ways to strive to make this Big Three a reality. Look, even Messer's. Bush and Putin fished together last week! Can you imagine American, Russian and Chinese military forces cooperating in the middle of a new Palestine, Israel and Lebanon – forcing the parties to peacefully negotiate a lasting settlement without daily bombs and rockets going off? The same for the Darfur region in Sudan. Wow! The UN Peacekeeping Forces could be doubled from 100,000 to 200,000, and its effectiveness increased tenfold. I know it may sound to some like a temporary occupation of foreigners in one sense, but mindsets can and must change if we finally want to end the killing! Armed groups killing in small groups or in mass will know their actions are not tolerated by the world community, that cultural values about violent behavior have changed, and that intervention consequences will be swift, harsh and certain. In a transitional period there would still be some killing of Man, but it would be the unfortunate few meeting their fate from the enforcers, not the innocents. The dream of Article 3 will become reality. The Rule of Law of Human Life will be enforced . . . all dependent on implementation of the next four interrelated steps as well.

2. NEW DIRECTIONS IN EDUCATION AND RESEARCH

Recent news reports cover the 23 killed and 160 wounded in bombs set off in Algeria. It also covered ABC's Diane Sawyer in Saudi Arabia asking young school children about Christianity and Islam, with one child saying Muslims are good and Christians are bad and another saying the reason being that Muslims pray and Christians do not. I recall my 18-year-old son visiting Communist Russia in 1983 and being handed a series of short books by his government guide on the great values of communism and socialism. So, the power of propaganda on our young minds. This is *education*?

Our Big Brain is so receptive for information. Those in power of any group try hard to impose their ideology on the minds of others, particularly upon the restless young. On the other hand, look now at the power of instant worldwide bits of information available on the World Wide Web. We are in a new "digital' age of the flow of bits of information at the speed of light in all kinds of electronic devices. All this in just the last twenty years of technology development. While we cannot necessarily find the Whole Truth in our exposure to all this available information, we certainly can find meaningful bits of it, and we certainly can expose our children of the world to the many sides of the same story. We can start with the fundamental that within each of us, as taught by religion or evolution, that each of us has the capacity for some "good" as well as the capacity for some "bad". We can teach and learn that peoples and cultures develop different patterns of thought and behavior to suit their advantageous needs at the time and that these cultures have the ability to adjust and grow as circumstances change. Values can change and improve. We can teach and learn that Man's Reason is a unique gift that allows our minds to unite upon what is "good", in this case the absence of Man killing Man to satisfy his angry emotions, his violent passions, his mindful obsessions, his intolerant beliefs, his excessive greed, and his conflicts with others. That justice can be achieved through peaceful means.

How do we find a practical way to move ahead in this educational endeavor with this wonderful new tool of electronic technology now available? How can we reach everyone? I suggest the United States take the lead and then present it to the United Nations for comment and electronic worldwide distribution. How difficult is Peace, even within the United States. It is common wisdom that if everyone capable of working has a job and meets his or her basic needs in a free society, the motivation for rebellion and violence is eliminated or greatly reduced. Yet look at the subway bombers in London or the alleged terrorists recently conspiring to attack Fort Dix, New Jersey – working minorities with no formal ties to radical Islamic terrorists in the Middle East. One of the New Jersey plotters indicated he did not care if he died: "We are all crazy", he stated. So then, let's start with the young and teach a mindset far removed from that concept.

My proposal to get started is for the United States Department of Education to appoint a commission comprised of a very diverse, cross sectional group of individuals to produce a simply written document, perhaps entitled "Mankind – Yesterday, Today and Tomorrow". It would contain *consensus representation from the scientific community, renowned philosophers, and the major religions* and would outline the histories of mankind, his various faiths, and the evolution of his major cultures. It would describe the major values from diverse cultures that have common sharing as well as major values not shared in common. It would highlight the role of aggression in the history of human development. Lastly, it would voice the positions of the smaller minority groups that are considered "radical" by the United Nations Commission on Human Rights.

This step is quite different than simply disseminating all the words of the UN's articles of human rights or if any other peace organization's. Thousands of individuals are unselfishly involved in these efforts with many good results. I simply want to go one step further by showing not only how we should behave but how and why we really do behave. This is an educational step, not and enforcement step. I believe once this simple message is available in both an emotional and rational format and read by or read to our six billion, we can then start to change mindsets, eventually leading to changes in behavior using the same tools of information creation and dissemination. I am not suggesting creating a system of "brainwashing", but one targeted only to the subject of willful violence. I am suggesting that once mankind has an exposure of our own commonalities and our differences, we will voluntarily agree that "killing one another is a bad thing", that its execution is not tolerated, and that the few who commit or who are willing to commit violence will be restrained.

Now does that air of restraint not sound like most individual communities in the world today which have local laws against physical assault and murder, have local police enforcement and have jails for the transgressors, the criminals? Yes, but with three important differences. One is that with New Directions in Education that broadly teach the basics of man's natures according to the best minds in science, religion and philosophy, New Directions in Research concerning better understanding the human brain and subsequent behavior, with the Refinement/Redirection of Competition and with New Initiatives in Conflict Resolution, we are going to witness less local violent crime in the first place. Secondly, with a stronger United Nations' role in policing civil and regional conflicts, we are going to witness fewer mass killings. Thirdly, the world community will join forces in resolving better ways to disarm radical terrorist groups committed to causes for which they are now willing to fight and die. *The great benefit of which will be the ability to expend more public resources towards peacefully ameliorating the other great problems of ample food supplies, water quality, disease management, and the education and training of the poorer peoples of the planet.* We all have heard the argument for less money on weapons and more on the human condition, but I suggest no such trend can take place without a major shift of mindsets away from willful violence.

In future essays, I will detail my suggestions on how to disseminate electronic and written documents to EVERYBODY! It is possible. In the US alone, it is estimated that from the ages of 12 to17, nearly 90% are already experiencing on line computer access to the Internet.

*   *   *

Let's turn to **RESEARCH**. Essay Two repeatedly referred to our physical big brain and its resulting mindfulness for EVERYTHING human! If that is so, what do we now know? My 1976 antique automobile still in my garage has no computer or electronic sensors. It burns a lot of gasoline. My 2004 model has sixty computerized sensors and controls and is much more fuel efficient. We have learned a lot in a short time about miniature electronics. I have a friend with diabetes taking human insulin grown in millions of bacterial cells. In just thirty years, the worlds of high tech computer electronics and high tech medical biotechnology have brought about incredible advances. In the medical world, we seem to be making big strides everywhere in knowledge about this human machine, *except about the brain*! My wife recently received an artificial hip joint to replace her disabled natural one. It works like a charm. Patients are now receiving transplanted kidneys and hearts. Cancer treatments, the most difficult of all, are steadily advancing.

However, in the brain fields of neuroscience, neurology, genetics, psychology, and psychiatry – I would call the strides steadily advancing but comparatively small. We are beginning to better understand our important brain chemicals and hormonal signals, and how they affect disorders and behaviors. We can better understand and better regulate too much dopamine, too little dopamine, too much serotonin and too little serotonin. As a recent edition of Time magazine highlighted, we have much better brain scan diagnostics now to locate damaged cells and show which areas of the brain are more or less active depending upon a particular stimulus. We have broadened our knowledge and treatment of neurotic and psychotic behaviors. We have added psychiatric clinical areas to our traditional hospitals, and we have expanded employer based mental health insurance coverage. On a limited basis, we have in the West become attracted to the East's mind/body approaches to well being, while the East seeks adoption of the high tech diagnostic and brain surgical procedures of the West. Lots of progress, but we are only scratching the surface. Our U.S center for government funded medical research, the National Institutes of Health, issued a report in May that it has studied children's brains using MRI scans and can conclude over which years our big brain grows the most. Interesting, but again this work is only scratching the surface. In the newer field of genetics, the entire human genome is being sequenced and a standard reference model constructed. However, already the leaders in the field are finding that they have greatly underestimated the extent of the genetic variation from one human to another.

My proposal is for a *major increase in NIH and university funding* for in depth studies of the brain's workings with our sensory systems, at the cellular level, at the neurotransmission level, and with the resulting control relationships with the body's chemical hormones that put us into action – into our behaviors. We need to learn a lot more in a hurry about this organ that controls mankind's destiny. How this biochemical physical organ creates this incredibly marvelous consciousness – what we call the mind. We need better explanations for the common expressions "crazy in the head" and "evil in the mind". We need to dramatically enhance this research effort, not just to understand and stop the killing among us, but as the best practical solution to bringing Reason to the forefront as a means to solving a host of Man's other daily life challenges – from disease to food production to water quality to environmental disasters. From this new direction, we will learn ways to continue to feel with our level 2 emotions but more universally and consistently act whenever appropriate with our level 3 reason. *I repeat my premise that level 2 emotions can trigger "good or bad guy" behavior but level 3 reasoning can trigger only "good guy" behaviors.* I know it is only my opinion, but as they say: trust me!! More detail in the next series of essays following up these FIVE STEPS.

3. MEDIA BLACKOUT OF WILLFUL VIOLENCE

Now comes the fun! Or should I say the hard part. Take on Hollywood? Free speech versus decency? Some behavioral psychologists arguing that witnessing deliberate human violence on television and in the movies is detrimental to children's future behavioral patterns. Other psychologists arguing that witnessing human deliberate violence on television and in the movies relieves internal pressures and is fine, just vicarious. After all, it's not "real" in horror producers' movies, but somehow it appears so "realistic" if treated as a historical production. Hollywood arguing the violence is simply "entertainment". Critics of violence arguing it's all about money. The rationale comes from all sides. The gun lobby arguing that people kill, not guns. Can we get anywhere near a consensus on these issues?

It does appear that anywhere in the world where both illicit drugs and illegal guns are easy to obtain there is a strong correlation to more violence. It does appear money is being made anywhere in the world by weapons suppliers, legally and illegally. Primitive armed camps used spears, bows and swords, originally to kill animals needed in the food supply, then against 'enemies". Now we witness armed camps and individuals possessing single shot handguns and rifles, automatic handguns and rifles, bombs, rockets, mortars, and WHAT'S NEXT? Radioactive materials? Germs?

If we retreat to and accept the two premises that (1) each Man has the innate, mostly recessed, capacity to kill his own kind when a particular set of perceived advantageous circumstances prescribe it, and (2) each Man has the unique brain capacity among all the mammals to reason, then I say let's move to the dual positions of both (A) further recessing that basic instinct and (B) further developing the function of using Reason as a tool against further perpetration of violence. That is a long sentence and hard to digest, but the meaning is essential to my point here. As a young man, Abraham Lincoln argued [in vain] for developing greater Reason in our civil affairs as our country slipped further away from the ideals of the 1776 Revolution and towards the unrelenting divisions that eventually culminated in our violent 1861 to 1865 Civil War. It is time to try again, and I realize that the impetus to change must begin with an *emotional* appeal as a prelude to a *reasonable* appeal as that is the sequence as to how our brain works.

I argue that "Hollywood" production needs a U-turn. Children and teenagers always seek new outlets for their immense energies and are easily impressed. Troubled adults not worried about eventual consequences of their actions find on screen examples of how to achieve their advantage, whether it's through excessive greed or mindless revenge. It is unrealistic to put all the responsibility for pre-adult behavior on the parents. The screens' "V" rating does not mean much. In the U.S., we are obviously not succeeding with so much "freedom" in producing and showing violent scenes. All of us see enough human suffering from natural tragedies – from accidents, hurricanes, tornados, and tsunamis and from realistic recordings of Man's history. Yet, is it not ironically interesting that two of the most popular TV programs of 2007 are one of dancing and one of singing. We do not have to show willful violence to be entertained! We need to and can change the MINDSET within our cultural values.

Our crisis is closely aligned to our two hundred year old founding documents in guaranteeing us rights to freedom of speech and to bear arms. Of course, while circumstances were much different then compared to the present day, I am not proposing we formally diminish those rights, just change their relative values. It is interesting to note how argumentative our forefathers were. How malicious were some of the words used in the practice of free speech. We should understand how necessary the need was then for armed citizens and militias when we did not yet have local and state police and suffered a history of tyranny. While we have no call to amend our Constitution, we do have call to smartly and with reason regulate the dangers in our society. For example, we now understand *with reason* the health dangers of smoking and regulate its use in public places. We understand *with reason* the jeopardy of citizens driving a powerful automobile on public roads without written and physical driving tests. Laws prescribed by governments allow but regulate these two practices both considered "rights". I know that even if we were to self-regulate guns through private registration societies and to self-regulate film and television production through private associations, I venture there would still be numerous critics on both sides. But I also venture the overwhelming majority of us would agree that taking steps away from the portrayal of violence would begin to change the mindset, and changing the mindset is a needed first step to the GOOD.

More about gun control laws, illegal guns and illicit drugs in future essays. My goal now is to convince the general entertainment media that it is to both their advantage and to Man's advantage to begin the process of the voluntary blacking out of willful acts of Man killing Man. A "V" rating becomes unnecessary for fictional and historical accounts because Man killing Man would not be explicitly shown. News is news and must be shown, but I pray the day the news will not have to show Man killing Man because it will not be happening on any common grand scale. The end of May 2007: the Hamas, the Fatah and the Israelites; the Lebanese army and the insurgents in the Palestinian refugee area; the Muslim sects and the Americans in Iraq; the factions in Pakistan; the Taliban in Afghanistan; rebels in Darfur and Nigeria. The more than 200 children and teenagers killed by bullets already this year in my native Philadelphia. One, on June 2nd, a teenager here dies from 12 bullets from pistols shot into him; on July 3rd, a 12 year old dies sitting in a car from stray rounds of a semi automatic rifle. The only hopeful news to me locally about the subject of violence concerns our likely next mayor, who after receiving criticism of his stop and search proposal of suspicious persons in high crime areas, expressed the view that he has **a civil right to life**. Now that is a good thought!

It is my strong opinion that changing the mindset away from willful violence begins with ending the views that fictional media productions of Man killing Man are fine for our subliminal brain health or fine for our enjoyment and entertainment. How we specifically do this is an action plan for future essays. It is time Man moves on. And sorry, Arnold, even your Man-looking machines are in for it.

4.   REFINEMENT/REDIRECTION OF COMPETITION

The concept of competition among and between Man is basic to our discussion. *Homo sapiens* were probably no different in behavior than the other mammals for hundreds of thousands of years. Competing for food supplies, competing for mates and competing for safe territories. Competing meaning striving for resources not everyone could possess at the same moment. The competition could have been in the form of verbal jabs, threatening positions, physical speed and endurance, mental manipulations, pushing, shoving, wounding and, yes, even killing within our own species *as a last resort*. As our big brain brought us the development of both better weapons and more useful resources, two basic conditions within societies began to evolve. War and Peace. Weapons development made brutal and violent competition for tangible resources easier to conduct for the stronger while on the other hand economic competition within and among cultures made mutually beneficial trading of resources easier to accomplish for the peaceful. Finally, further development of our big brain at last brought us both violent and peaceful competition over intangible ideas – the "fight" over which minds had sole claim to the "right" religious, philosophic, economic, political and subjective cultural values. In my lifetime, I cannot think of an example of a more violent outcome over the competition of gaining new tangible resources through the use of war while at the same time subscribing to an intangible idea of defending one's native culture than the battle for the eight square mile Iwo Jimo. Of the 22,000 Japanese troops defending the island, 20,000 perished while the American toll was 7,000. Incredible!

Today, we see daily signs of our most basic instincts everywhere, the two poles often melding together in a blur. We see competition resulting from our "aggressive" basic instinct; we see cooperation from our "compassionate" basic instinct. We hear calls for "fight em", "go get em", as well as calls for "help them". We see in America the redirection of our aggressive competitive instinct into contact sports like football, ice hockey, wrestling and boxing, and then we see less physically aggressive non-contact sports like golf and tennis competitions. We see a very refined competition into awards for best in art, literature, dance, music and school grades. Leaning to the other side, we see compassionate cooperation as we look at so many dedicated individuals working in hospitals, private charitable organizations and governmental social agencies. We go all the way to the one side to the gun toting drug criminals competing for power over drug distribution to all the way the other side to socially isolated advocates of pure love and total peace.

Within these wide extremes, mainstream moderate Americans practice a nice blend of everyday peaceful competitive activities with everyday cooperative undertakings. Such is the peaceful blend of instinctive and cultural behaviors of most of our citizens, enforced by our law and order codified values. It brings out the best in us! So then, what's the problem in America? Just rope off those inner city violent areas where an overabundance of illicit drugs and illegal guns prevails? No, because there are too many innocent persons caught in the middle, and the problem is more widespread than just inner cities. No, because there are too many caring persons that have to deal with the damages to life and property. No, because the numbers of unnecessary guns and illicit brain damaging drugs are increasing. No, because in my opinion the mental images of such violent behavior in the media motivate more of such behavior in the general population. No, because our American cultural value is 99.9999% accepted that absent defensive war and pure self-defense, Man should not kill Man, and in fact, that absent contact sport, Man should not even physically push or shove another Man.

Thus in the total scope of things, I see two general scenarios: the first groups the many countries around the world with cultural values and social situations generally compatible with the United Nations Charter; and the second groups those countries around the world where willful violence is fostered, accepted or commonplace. In both cases, in addition to the simultaneous implementation of the other four Steps I am submitting, this Step involves further refinement in the first group and a redirection in the second group of the competitive forces at work in these societies.

* * *

Before specifically presenting my ideas for how and why we should redirect competition, let me digress. All this "explanation" of mine about Man and his place in the universe of course has been well thought out in philosophy, interpretive art, and religion long before. We know the names of the mindful Aristotle and Plato from twenty four hundred years ago, to the religio-philosophic Tao, Buddha, Confucius, Abraham, Jesus and Muhammad. We know the names Michelangelo and daVinci from the artistic 15th century Renaissance period. We know the names Newton, Voltaire, Rousseau, Locke, Kant and Smith from the 18th century Age of Science, Enlightenment and Reason. Later to the vast influences of Darwin, Marx and Einstein. What I find interesting is that all these brilliant minds seemed to center upon one basic premise that was new or relatively new at that time. A definitive, incredibly persuasive position was taken without invoking too much interrelationship with other behavioral forces at work. Violent conflict continued as part of the norms of the day.

In the West, art and expression flourished during the Renaissance period, but they mostly related to religious meaning. Newtonian thoughts followed, with a strong bent towards explaining the seemingly natural laws of the physical world. The age of Enlightenment and Reason subsequently sought understanding of Man's place and role in the natural world by using the reasoning power of his mind over the mystical beliefs of religion. This philosophy believed Man to be basically good by nature, and that with education Man could improve his lot if left in a state of freedom from the oppressions of the church and the monarchial state. Such was the advocacy of the Voltaires' and the Kants'. As would be expected, opposing reactions developed – from Rousseau's distrust of reason to his advocacy of emotion and intuition in guiding behavior and to the church's new more humanitarian role in society. The Catholic Church of the West split into many competitive factions. Who and What ruled? Was it the heart, the mind, or the supernatural? Each advocate took a position. In the Middle East, religious scholar after scholar tried reinterpreting the true meaning of the Koran while witnessing the continued stress of sect versus sect within Islam, with competition for the "right" ideas still continuing today. Is Jihad the peaceful striving of the individual for improvement, or is it the group striving for war against nonbelievers? In the East, the followers of the ancient Buddha continued to move towards rational, even scientific, explanations for their belief in the quest for compassion.

*　　*　　*

With this background involving Man's intellect, one can understand the reasons for his growing population and dominance among the mammals despite periodic famines, diseases and wars. Competition in the intellectual realm bred all kinds of new outcomes. As science and technology advanced ever more rapidly, and industry trade and commerce accelerated the trend away from agricultural employment, competition over the "best" economic systems became the basis of national ideological political systems – capitalism, socialism, and communism. In all this incredible pace of change and argument, one factor remained – Man's capacity to kill his fellow man. The wars of the 20th Century were massive in scope. Technical advances in weaponry and transportation combined with stubborn clinging to the righteousness of a national ideological position resulted in competition among Man's beliefs becoming actualized in its most brutal form, that is, World War, a calamity overriding Man's counterbalancing forces of love and compassion. This narrative brings one back to the beginning point of my essays. After all this diversity of philosophical beliefs has been examined, after all this diversity in religious sects has been exposed, after all this science has been discovered right up to the mapping of the human genome, after all these wars between and among nation states have been recorded by historians and the media, would one not think that Man at this stage would at the very least keep his competitive state, his striving for advantage, non violent? My humble intellect, my mind, my consciousness is not powerful enough to arrive at a conclusion as to how Man should live his life. I am not suggesting a New World Order. Just look at all those great intellects of the last 2500 years that I previously mentioned and see that not one of them can lay claim to ruling either the hearts or minds of all our six billion populace. We may have significant blocs of select believers and followers to a particular creed, but we are far from unanimous. Remember each of us has a controlling mechanism, our big brain, which is similar in structure but slightly different in microscopic genetic mix. Moreover, it doesn't always operate in action according to the basic blueprint's design. Nonetheless, let us refine the not impossible task to redirect human competition, that striving for individual or group advantage over conditions and resources, in a mutually beneficial way without the threat or use of willful violent behavior.

Accordingly, I submit Step Four as introducing a *New Age of Reason*. Yes, another "Age". The element of competition might be called a new international, national or individual "game". It does not conflict with the theories of modern science or major religions or major philosophies. It simply argues that man is complex and diverse, having capacities for good and bad, that religions are wonderfully beneficial most of the time yet based upon mystical hope and faith, that science improves the condition of Man most of the time, but that religion and science still have vast unresolved issues and many mysteries. It argues that while the organization of human activities into different forms of economic, political and social systems do not always produce equal and mutually beneficial standards for the human condition, that there are explainable reasons for such grounded in our many different human natures. It argues that while caring and compassion are common advantageous qualities universal in Man's instinctive qualities, so is competition a universal instinctive trait. It is a natural force that drives Man towards an advantage over another which at times can be overtly aggressive – to the point of violent behavior. Think of this: confronted with conflict it is very easy, due to wide availability and simplicity of use, to instigate the competitive action of carrying a gun to secure a personal advantage, while it is often much more difficult for the instinctive trait of compassion to carry out a behavioral act of caring to secure a mutual advantage. In other words, is it not easier to espouse a position and protect it with weapons; is it not more difficult to espouse and protect with words? The non-violent influences of the likes of Mahatma Gandhi's and Martin Luther King's are few and far between. Let's agree – conviction of the certainty of whatever one's beliefs can be a virtue, but not to the point of imposing it upon others with the use of violence.

In *societies where rulers generally fair to all are the norm*, human violence is relatively low. Accordingly, there we are on the right track in promoting more and more friendly competition balanced with more and more ways of cooperative caring. Sports, arts, music, dancing, academics, business and commerce are some of the many activities that allow the competitive instinct to flourish and result in significant human achievement. Participation in social aid, health services and charitable organizations are some of the many activities that allow our compassionate instincts to flourish and also result in significant human accomplishment. Accordingly, in these societies in a New Age of Reason, we can amend our values by adopting a complete intolerance to willful human violence and refine our competitive activities by "getting everyone able into the game". In the United States it seems as though we have lot of players but what is the percentage playing full time? In our schools, what percentage of students participates in after school hours' sports, music and clubs? As adults, what percentage has a real voice in their occupation? What percentage watch passively at others competing and caring as opposed to participating? It is not surprising how little frustrations in American life can boil over into inappropriate behavior.

For my part, I will be searching for concrete solutions as to how we get everyone in the game. I know teenage violence can be reduced substantially, not only by educating about its consequences, or by reducing their number of illegal guns and illicit drugs, but by getting all kids busy after normal school hours. I know the argument against will be lack of funding, but I think I have a way. Refining the element of competition in America and elsewhere is a Step that can be achieved. And to the constructive good for all will be other ways to keep our energetic young growing into "good" citizens, such as compulsory pre-school "brain" development and a Year of National Service after high school– to be discussed later. Libertarians do not be concerned – I am referring to children and teens.

In those societies where violence is commonplace, a more fundamental redirection of competition is required. As I have proposed, the first Step is the establishment of law and order even if it takes the new UN SuperForce to accomplish it. But I have an important difference. The traditional world now states to the "bad guys": 'turn in your guns, renounce violence, and we'll negotiate", while the progressive world just says "let's talk". My approach is broader in that all Five Steps need to be in motion simultaneously. The "bad guys" need to see that they can obtain an advantage without resorting to violence[Step Five], that violence is universally intolerable and punishable[Step One], that through electronic education and new research into behavior[Step Two], their particular set of needs or injustices can be reconciled with the mainstream and that means can be found to redirect their competitive abilities into positive advantages[Step Four].

In practical terms at this point in our history, we quickly and dramatically need these Steps introduced into the Islamic communities that are experiencing significant violence among themselves, with Israel, within Lebanon, Russia/Chechnya and several African nations, and with the West in general. It is fine to target the so-called War on Terror as against only a small number of extreme Islamists who are motivated to kill anyone opposed to their narrow view as to how society should be organized. But for 1400 years and to the present day, the problem is much larger in scope. Like Christianity four hundred years ago, Islam as a religion is undergoing a major transformation within. Where do women fit in? What is the "right" line of succession of Muhammad? Does the personal striving message of Jihad have to include the conversion or killing of nonbelievers, the infidels? Must the national government be secular [Turkey] or theocratic [Iran]? Can Jewish Israel peacefully coexist with Muslim Palestine when residents both claim the same historic lands or even the same houses? Can Christians share political positions in Islamic dominated societies? Can Arab descent Muslims coexist economically on fair terms with African descent Muslims? Do disenfranchised Muslim youth have to take up the call to arms at the beckon of extreme thinking adults if it means becoming a suicide bomber with the promise of a direct path to Paradise? Can strict obedience to the word of God as thought to be heard by Muhammad ever be reconciled with the free thoughts of an atheist or with the media images of a Western culture laden with drugs and explicit sex?

At a time when it becomes increasingly easy to conceal small weapons of mass destruction, we Man need to confront this issue with our collective full force. On this issue right now, redirecting our evolutionary, or cultural, or God given capacity for destructive competitive behavior is essential. It can be done. Christian divisions in Europe still argue but no longer physically fight; formerly physically aggressive German and Japanese societies are now peaceful and prosperous. **URCV. Use Reason, Change Values!** Muslims can maintain their most important traditional peaceful convictions yet still debate their values and differences among themselves, with Israel, with the West and with the East, but the entire world must come together to achieve this goal by *eliminating any value attached to violence*.

*   *   *

My initial direction in the more troubled areas would be twofold: while the Five Steps are being taken simultaneously, have the world community through the revamped UN contribute financially to actively employing young men and women of these target nations into both the peacekeeping forces and the care giving forces within their native countries. This step gets them prideful busy into building their own societies in a nonviolent, caring fashion. Secondly, backed by the peacekeeping UN SuperForce, engage the World Bank and other international economic institutions to help redirect competition in these nations into building industries that gainfully employ residents. We have witnessed economic miracles in Taiwan, in South Korea and in Shanghai, China. The next examples could be a competitive exportable farm product for the Afghan poppy field growers [interesting that opium production in Afghanistan has risen 70% since the US drove off the Taliban from power and that much of the opium derivatives are consumed by US drug users], or petroleum industry sub-industries in Nigeria where the benefit of oil exporting revenues are now concentrated among a powerful few and violence is prevalent. The Palestinian teenagers and young adults in the Gaza strip. What is their product?

Some might argue we in the US are losing our ability to reason as we are increasingly "manipulated" by television sound bites. I would argue that a New Age of Reason is open to more of us, as opposed to just the intellectual few of former days. And I would argue that we all still need that Level 2 Emotion daily. It gives us feelings of joy, of elation, of fun, of excitement, of yearning, of crying, of sorrow, of beauty, of warm ambience. We just all need to open up the capacity of our Level 3 Reason – the brainpower to use mindful, rational, non-emotional patterns of thought to solve our most pressing problems even though agreement among us is difficult. Ben Franklin's newspapers were full of half truths, and Hamilton and Jefferson fought bitterly over our nation's well being and direction. General Douglas McArthur was fired by President Truman for his ideas for winning the Korean War. President Bush sinks in the polls despite his plea for expanding democracies and that man's nature is to seek liberty. Arguments won, arguments lost.

True to our natures, emotions usually win out as they directly promote behavioral actions. Reason is often in the mind of the passive beholder. The point is that not a lot has been, is, or will be changing about our basic human natures. Disagreements will continue to abound. Rodney King's bewilderment as to why we can't all get along as he was being dragged off to jail is not such a puzzle after all. However, the point also is that through our reasoning ability we do have the collective capacity to agree to value life and to agree to devalue the willful taking of another's life. We cannot quickly change our genes, but we can amend our cultural values and find specific ways to decrease violently aggressive behavior by refining and redirecting the role of competition among us. Whether in the realm of competition for tangible resources or over intangible ideologies, violence is out!

Nice footnote here: on July 29 the Iraqi national soccer team won the Asian Cup and citizens of Iraq united in joy – Sunni, Shiite, Kurd and Christian. Ah, peaceful competition!

5. NEW INITATIVES IN CONFLICT RESOLUTION

You are in the United States of America. Suppose you do not like the way the boss is running the company. He favors his cronies, and you do not think you are being paid fairly. You protest, but he does not listen. You become verbally disruptive with other employees and adversely affect their work performance. The boss fires you. Following the normal values of our culture, he does not shoot you, and you do not shoot him. You are temporarily disgruntled but able in our free society to find another job. You have a friend in another company who is a member of the union there, and his grievance was heard by a committee of union and company representatives, and part of his problem was corrected to his advantage. You have another friend who had a similar problem to yours in a very enlightened company. Working with his company's Human Resource Department, a reasonable arrangement was diligently worked out to both your friend's advantage and to the company's.

Now on a factual basis, recall that postal worker in a Southern California town that allowed a grievance with his boss to so upset his fragile mind that he lost mental control and proceeded to behave outside the norms, the values, the rules of his culture. He obtained a gun, returned to the post office and shot ands killed twenty of his former co-workers. Fortunately, this kind of event is uncommon in America, but does happen. In fact, it even happens in our schools – Columbine, Amish Pennsylvania, and Virginia Tech. Thousands of conflicts of all proportions happen everyday. Many are resolved, or allowed to simmer, or they just go away. A few become violent. Understanding the workings of the brain, we understand these happenings. Emotion over reason to the extreme. Rational becoming irrational in the disturbed mind.

Now let's leave America and go all the way to the West Bank. Who originally among the tribes of Man lived there? The Jewish religion was practiced there beginning some four thousand years ago. Abraham. The Jews dispersed, returned, and dispersed again. Many Arabs living there became Muslims after Muhammad's revelations in the seventh century A.D. The lands were contested among followers of these two religions. After World War II, the nation of Jordan administered the West Bank territory where mostly Arab Muslims lived while the new United Nations created the new nation of Israel for the Jews to the West Bank's west, north and south. The Arabs objected, fought and lost their 1948 war with Israel. Syria, Jordan and Egypt tried again in 1967 to invade Israel but lost again. Israel then expanded its borders to better protect its borders and took over authority for the West Bank. In 1992, the Palestinians regained civil and security control of selected areas of the West Bank. Many Arabs living there crossed daily into Israel for gainful employment. Some Arabs living in Israel became citizens of Israel. Slowly but surely, some Israelis moved their homes into new Jewish settlements in the West Bank. Sound complicated? Intractable?

Some elements among the Palestinian people continue to offer violent opposition to the concept of an Israel. The Israelis then fight back. It appears the nations of the world and perhaps the majorities of the Palestinian and Jewish peoples would like a peaceful two-nation existence, but how to create it is vexing to everyone. The situation is one big, historic, religious, cultural, emotional mix. A classic confrontation subject to continuing waves of failed reconciliation and repeated violence. No one has an answer? I am a Palestinian youth living in the West Bank with no job, no country. My father was killed by an Israeli tank coming into my territory in search of a cell of suicide bombers. I am now an Israeli youth living with my parents in the West Bank with a job and a country, but my brother had been killed in a crowded market by a suicide bomber and my sister was killed by a Palestinian rocket lobbed into our backyard when we use to live near the Lebanon border. How in the world could these two young men ever come together and settle their conflict without trying to kill each other. Their instinctive competition for their secure home turf is as basic and as intense as it can get. From their past personal tragedies to their present condition, they shout emotionally at each other, then they cool down and list their grievances. They both conclude they are getting nowhere. They both wish to live in their same historic land area, but they practice different religions and live under separate political rule. There appears to be no way that either is going to give in his position. Neither budges. Talk is cheap, rockets impact. The emotion of revenge fills the air. How understandable becomes this thrust of human violence.

*   *   *

History is full of violent uprisings and revolutions against repressive leaders and governments. At the time, there was no other way. Yet more recently, the human mind does find creative ways to have grievances aired, fences mended and future generations spared from bloodshed. Japanese children and American children of parents lost at each other's hands during WW II are not at odds. Early union-company conflicts

58

witnessed many incidents of protests turned violent. Eventually unionization became accepted and protected by the laws of the land. Grievance procedures were established, and conflicts were resolved through negotiation, mediation and arbitration practices. Unresolved conflicts were settled without bloodshed through the economic forces of legalized strikes by union members and legal lockouts and relocations by management. Sometimes companies closed or moved; sometimes employees had to retrain for other jobs elsewhere, but the point is we learned not to resort to violence.

Today, American business practices are generally marked with open economic competition, conflict resolution fair to all, employee retraining, employer flexibility and penalties for unethical behavior. The American business engine at times produces some excesses and some abuses, and with changing business conditions will always have parts to fix. But it is an economic machine that has produced more goods, services and benefits for each of its participants than any system ever devised. The learning curve is that *new initiatives in conflict resolution can be transitioned from the American business experience to the world stage of conflict resolution in other matters* – especially into the world of violence. How to accomplish?

First, applied to America, let's take violence in our schools and among teenage street gangs. My Mom, it's a fact, taught school in inner city Philadelphia for thirty years. Assaults against teachers by students were fundamentally unheard of then, but now I read that the current school year recorded some 1500! I will be striving in the coming months to add to the mix of current good intentions and practices among government programs and civic leaders in their efforts to curb violence with a number of specific proposals in enhancing their efforts. Measurable win-win propositions are achievable if successful community businesses with good human relations practices are added to the mix. More later in the next Mind Set Essays of the Humanity Series.

Second, envision in the world international hotspots we have [1] a new UN strength in enforceable peacekeeping; [2] we have new directions in mass education and behavioral research; [3] we have new positive assistance from the visual media; [4] we have ways of redirecting competition to more fruitful purposes. And now [5], we have new initiatives in conflict resolution where a weapon is not the final arbiter. Can you imagine right now in July 2007 the United States is negotiating the selling of advanced weapons to certain Middle East nations as a way to counter the assumed threat of an aggressive Iran? We are on a merry-go-round!

Through a *new initiative* led by the top US schools of business in coalition with top business schools of the other G8 member nations – Canada, Britain, Germany, France, Russia and Japan – new protocols will be developed in coordination and cooperation with the G8 state department leaders and corresponding UN ambassadors. For instance, the practice of sanctions will be modified where it has been used to ignore and isolate a nation, hoping the people there will rise and overthrow a repressive government. Economic sanctions and isolation of Cuba have left its citizens disadvantaged and Castro still in power almost fifty years later. Same with North Korea. Limited sanctions are unlikely to be successful in Nigeria as long as the US and China buy so much of that country's crude oil output. Limited sanctions applied to Iran appear so far to have minor success where state theology is backed by the military. Sanctions surely did not work during the 1990's against Iraq as militarily protected Saddam Hussein used "oil for food" revenues to his own purposes and not to the benefit of his country's Shia southern region. We read and hear over and over from some advocates that we must negotiate, not fight, with our adversaries, but the essence to successful negotiations is bringing the most current best practices and detailed techniques to the negotiating tables.

So, what works and what doesn't work? Raw strength and pure weakness result in win-lose outcomes that allow the conflict to continue later. Agreements reached will be breached. Nor can balancing strength and weakness with mutual weapons any longer be the best game in town. The American business school mentality of gaining a strong competitive advantage does not mean putting all the other players out of the game. No competition in time becomes unfair to suppliers, to employees and to customers and eventually ends the game. It's called unfair monopoly. Unfair trade practices against business competitors are regulated by the umpire – local, state and federal laws enacted by representatives of the people. Nor does the concept work of having every player in the game the same – experience has revealed that inefficiency. What does work is positive resolution of conflict with members of one's own team as essential to the long-term success of one's business and competing on terms where all the players strive for and enjoy some varying degree of mutual advantage.

Very orderly this massive, competitive world business economy. How do we expect these advanced conflict resolution practices to be introduced and enforced in the violent hot spots around the world? Certainly we cannot expend citizens' money and energy to help produce win-win situations proving an advantage to all parties involved in the conflict and then not have the means to back it up. We are an incredibly split nation now as to what to do about the internal strife among armed competing factions in Iraq. We have 160,000 troops there! We are also assisting the diverse peoples of Kosovo and Serbia to negotiate peacefully in determining the fate of their region – Kosovo to be autonomous or to be part of Serbia. To allow this process to advance and prevent further violence in this conflict, there have been fifteen thousand American troops there for almost ten years! We need to learn how to enhance this process to come to speedier accords. Once accomplished, can we then utilize this technique in other troubled spots? The answer is yes. We can and we must.

Recent enhancing of the UN force now at the Lebanon/Israel border is a holding operation. The violence has stopped temporarily, but the conflict is not moving towards resolution. The new initiative: placing 15,000 American troops along side 15,000 Russian along side 15,000 Chinese in Lebanon/ Israel/Palestine under the UN banner is half the action plan; the other half is the UN/G8 negotiating team that will help teach the sides how to reach accommodating *mutual advantages to all parties with appropriate incentives* for doing so. I see this as not a criticism of the various state departments and country ambassadors now trying their best, but as an important enhancement in helping them accomplish their difficult tasks. Only then can that Palestinian boy and that Israeli boy feel safe together and gainfully move on with their lives, their religions and their respective countries.

In cooperation with the UN full membership, its Security Council, the new UN SuperForce, and the new UN/G8 Negotiating Team, the international community will find the funds and volunteers to accomplish this great endeavor. There is so much competition already for sufficient funds to battle other major problems such as natural disasters, famine and disease, but *the major benefit of virtually eliminating Man killing Man will be the freeing of significant funds, the freeing of the element of fear, and the great enhancement of our marvelous human gift – Man's Reasoning Power – to better solve all those other problems Man faces.*

*   *   *

In conclusion, this first part of my Humanity Essay Series is an attempt to explain why human violence still persists when it seems almost everyone avows to be against it, and it is a call for action to promote new steps in solving what seems to be an ageless drag on advancing the human condition. I see no reason why we cannot achieve success! The Five Steps are EMOTIONALLY IRRESISTIBLE AND LOGICALLY SOUND!

www.ingramcontent.com/pod-product-compliance
Lightning Source LLC
Chambersburg PA
CBHW021548290526

45784CB00016B/2430

To arrange speaking engagements for
Tyrone Everett at your church or fellowship
contact 904-282-8510 or email
TYNCHRIST4U@YAHOO.COM